An Introduction to Broom grass Cultivation:

A potential multipurpose future Crop

of North-Eastern India

By

SIBDAS BASKEY

BIBLAP TUDU

NIRANJAN MANDI

1

Content at a glance

Globally broom cultivation has made a phenomenal progress. The growth of this multipurpose plant also has changed dramatically in the recent past due to crop improvement advancement in production technology. In India North Eastern Himalayan range is enriched with many valuable herbs and superior genotype. Himalaya is known for its rich and diverse plant wealth from time immemorial. The diversity of this resource is quite pronounced both horizontally and vertically. The Darjeeling Himalaya harbors a diverse genotype of broom grass and it is used as the herbal medicinal practices by among all ethno-cultural groups of this region. Broom grasses are already exploited at a large scale which is going to be threatened their existence due to harvesting before pollination and for making soft broom which fetches good price. The status of this plant in the context of their existence, exploitation and usage requires considerable attention due to its alarming depletion of population. There is huge demand of this herb in market so an immediate attention towards documentation of the status, usage and potential in this of this plant is required.

Concerted research efforts are being made by the scientists around the world to adopt, apply and evaluate the methodology for conservation of this herb and improving crop yield. Understanding and prediction of crop response to environment is the major theme which may further help to identify improved crop management practices.

This book is a mixture of theoretical and applied investigation together with a number of studies of current research programmes and innovative and successful crop cultivation strategies done in Regional Research Centre (Hill Zone), UBKV, Kalimpong along its adjoining parts like Lava, Pedong Algarah, etc. The focus is on conservation and increase in population of this endangered with certain improved management techniques. The book is the result of a collective effort of scientist from various disciplines of this institution. The output made by the scientist will serve as a valuable reference for researchers, teachers and student. We will be happy if the book will ultimately serve the purpose of scientists, educational researchers, farmers and different companies engaged in research work and commercial cultivation of this valuable endangered plant in a meaningful way.

Sibdas Baskey

Biblap Tudu

Niranjan Mandi

Acknowledgement

Broom grass, an important multipurpose plant of Himalaya has become a subject of great interest recently. First of all, fervently and modestly we express our deep sense of gratitude to (Prof. (Dr.) Debashis Mojumder, Honourable Vicc-chancellor for his keen interest and moral support for the preparation of this manuscript regarding outcome of various research findings of this herb.

'We are immensely grateful to Prof. Ashok Choudhury, Director of Research, for his valuable advice and thought provoking suggestion, which greatly help us to develop a keen research aptitude regarding this valuable plant and develop this manuscript in a fruitful way.

'We express our sincerest and heart felts gratitude to Dr. Jitendra Kumar, Director, ICAR-Directorate of Medicinal and Aromatic Plants for his valuable guidance, keen and continued interest, encouragement with constructive suggestions throughout the course of research work which ultimately helped us to infer our research findings.

The support and hard work provided by the staff members of AICRP on MAP& B is highly acknowledged. Our special thanks to Forest officers (DFO) and Range officer, whose immense experience and Knowledge, we have utilized in ample measures to build up the broom grass information base. This work would not have been possible without the co-operation of the people living in the area who helped us during the field visits.

The help extended by the scientists of the Regional Research Station (Hill Zone), Kalimpong are gratefully acknowledged. We are extremely grateful to the ADR, UBKV (HZ), Kalimpong, Darjeeling for generous financial assistance for this programme.

Sibdas Baskey

Biblap Tudu

Niranjan Mand

Introduction

Broom grass, Thysanolaena maxima (Roxb.) Kuntze, (family—Poaceae), is an important perennial grass and grows in almost all parts of South and Southeast Asia up to an elevation of 2,000 m and climatic conditions ranging from tropical to subtropical. Its inflorescence used to make broom which is locally known as *Phool jhadu*. It is a fast growing plant will grow well in either full sun or part shade. It grows wild in the hills of the northeastern region of India and in Darjeeling and Sikkim Himalayas. It is usually planted during April-May and the culms are arising centrifugally during the peak growth period (June-July) and bear inflorescence at the end of vegetative growth. The inflorescence becomes ready for harvest by December-January and harvest continues until March (Bisht and Ahlawat, 1998).Broom grass forms tussocks. The tussocks (plants) of broom grass are then cleared of old tillers since each tiller produces panicles only once. The yield of broom panicles is reported to be highest during the 3rd and 4th year of the plant age and thereafter the production gradually decline up to 6th year, It should be re-transplanted after 6th year . In North eastern states, broom grass was introduced by the state forest department about three decades ago under a silvi-pastoral system in social forestry plantations for generating income during gestation periods i.e. periods between plantation and harvest of timber. Now, the plant has been domesticated and cultivated on large scale by hill farmers. The broom made out of the inflorescence of this plant is sold across South and Southeast Asia and the market is expanding in India, Nepal, Bangladesh, China, Japan and Middle East. One hectare yields US$503 (Vernon, 2006).Annual Indian broom market estimate is US$60M (Shankar *et. al.,* 2001).1 ton of flowers processed into soft brooms fetch about US$1,333 (Bhuchar, 2008). Worth of flowers increases up to 2.65 times if processed into soft brooms (Fetalvero *et. al.,* 2011).Return on Investment is 1.7 times of the total investment (Bhuchar, 2008).

The demand of broom have increased manifold in the last two decades. Now, Broom grass cultivation is a viable option to get high profit as having high market demand due to decreasing production in natural forests. It is a multipurpose grass. Inflorescence(Panicle) used for broom making, The leaves and tender shoots are used as fodder, stems are used as raw material in paper industries, dry stems are used as fuel, support sticks in crop fields for trailing crops, mulching materials and small-scale cottage industries for making mats.

It is important both economically and ecologically for the farming community of Darjeeling Himalaya. It could become an effective component for rural development in the northeastern states as its cultivation needs minimum input and labour and generates a very attractive economic return .Vast areas of wastelands can be used to ensure conservation of soil and water, at the same time, enhancing the livelihood of the rural poor in the country by adopting large-scale cultivation.

Part I: General aspects

1. **Botanical Name:** Thysanolaena maxima (Roxb.) Kuntze (1891)

   Synonyms

   Melica latifolia Roxb. ex Hornem. (1819),

   Agrostis maxima Roxb. (1820),

   Thysanolaena latifolia (Roxb. ex Hornem.) Honda

   Common names

   Tiger grass, Broom grass,Asian broom grass, Clumping grass (**English**).

   India: Jono_ak (Santali), Phul-jaru, jharu-Ghash (Bengali),Amliso (Nepali)

   Indonesia: Awis (Sundanese), Menjalin Wuwu (Javanese), Lantebung (Makasar).

   Malaysia: Buloh Teberau, Rumput Buloh.

   Philippines: Tambu (Tagalog), Gatbo (Bikol), Buybuy (Ilokano).

   Laos: kheem khoong.

   Thailand: Tongkong, Laolaeng (Northern), Ya-yung (Southern).

2. Origin and geographic distribution

Tiger grass grows from India to Indo-China and China and throughout south-east Asia. It is also occasionally cultivated outside this region. It occurs in temperate and sub-tropical parts of India especially Meghalaya, Assam, Arunachal Pradesh, Mizoram, Sikkim, Nicobar Islands, West Bengal (Darjeeling), Tripura, Bangladesh, Bhutan, Myanmar, Malayasia, Indonesia, Japan, Laos, Sri Lanka, Thailand, Vietnam, Philipines, China, East Asia, Nepal, New Guinea and Malaysia up to 2000 m above mean sea level.

Biogeography of Broom grass

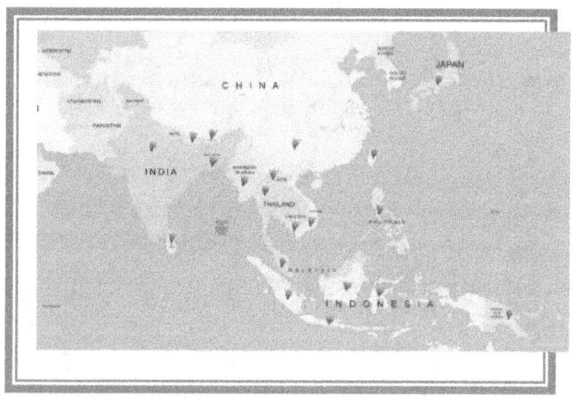

(Source: Fetalvero, E. G., 2012)

Habit and Habitat

Tiger grass is evergreen, tall, rhizomatous and tufted perennial grass. It has solid, smooth and rounded culms. Grass clump is in tussock (bunch) form, Culms arise centrifugally, green when young, brownish green at maturity.

It naturally colonizes areas with newly exposed soils due to land slide, road sides, abandoned quarries, abandoned jhum (shifting cultivation) areas, and waste lands. It grows below 2,000m a.m.s.l. on a wide range of agro-climatic conditions in varying soils type, in shady hill slopes, rocky soil structure, damp steep river banks, and valleys. Large areas of abandoned jhum fields have also been converted to broom grass plantations in the last two decades, due to an increase in demand for brooms from various parts of the country.

3. Production levels in National and International

Now, Broom grass cultivation is getting momentum from India to Indo-China and China and throughout south-east Asia. It is also occasionally cultivated outside this region. It is adopted for cultivation in temperate and sub-tropical parts of India especially Meghalaya, Assam, Arunachal Pradesh, Mizoram, Sikkim, Nicobar Islands, West Bengal (Darjeeling), Tripura, and neighboring country like Bangladesh, Bhutan, Myanmar, Malayasia, Indonesia, Japan, Laos, Sri Lanka, Thailand, Vietnam, Philipines, China, East Asia, Nepal, New Guinea and Malaysia up to 2000 m above mean sea level. The broom made out of the inflorescence of this plant is sold across South and Southeast Asia and the market is expanding in India, Nepal, Bangladesh, China, Japan and Middle East. One hectare yields US$503 (Vernon, 2006).Annual Indian broom market estimate is US$60M (Shankar et al., 2001).1 ton of flowers processed into soft brooms fetch about US$1,333 (Bhuchar, 2008).

4. Major Production area in India

Broom grass is one of the major cash crop in Arunachal Pradesh,Sikkim, Darjeeling district of West Bengal,Tripura, Meghalaya and other North-eastern States. One who has travelled in the hill-roads of North-east in winters must have been amused by its beautiful inflorescence dotting the hillsides. In 2013-14, farmers alone have earned an income of Rs 226.54 lakh and the total volume of collection was 459 metric ton from broom grass. If harvesting managed scientifically, an estimated 6000 metric-ton of the grass can be harvested annually from Tripura's forests alone. However, Meghalaya has now emerged as one of the largest producers and exporters of broom grass in the country. Ninety percent of the brooms produced are exported outside the State. The production of brooms in Meghalaya, from 2004 to 2009, shows that there is a trend of increase in production, price, and growers' income. This may be attributed to the expanding market for the product.

5. Description of Plant

A perennial, handsome, tufted grass. Culms are rounded, solid, reed-like erect or ascending, 2.5-3.5m. tall with glabrous nodes and leaf-sheaths at least the upper ones, tight, glabrous, terete, smooth, the nodes glabrous, margins with some short stiff hairs towards the throat. Leaves are large, broad, lanceolate, narrowed into an acuminate apex, base semi-amplexicaul, 30-60X5-7cm. glabrous, ligule a shallow membrane 1-2 mm deep, backed by short stiff hairs. Panicles are effuse, decompounds, glabrous, 35-60 cm. long with fili-form branches. Spikelets are greenish or purplish, 2-flowered, 1-2 nate, elliptical, minute, lanceolate, acuminate, pedicillate, numerous, often in pairs on a common peduncle, each pedicel distinct. Involucral glume is hyaline and sub-equal. Lower floral glume is empty and lanceolate whereas, upper one is hermaphrodite, ciliate with erect, ovate, white, long hairs. stigmata 2, plumose; reddish brown, the rachilla continues as a flattened process with an expanded tip, beyond and behind the upper lemma. The aspect of the spikelets changes with the onset of anthesis when the upper lemma emerges and its setose hairs gradually adopt a stance at right angles to the lemma's surface. Flowering and fruiting period is November and March respectively.

Morpho-anatomy of Broom Grass

Figure:1

Growth and development

In light shade seedlings grow slowly at first, but are then able to compete with other low-growing plants. It grows wild in deep forest, river and stream banks, rocks and uncultivable lands in foothills up to 2000 m. above Mean sea level. As a crop it does well without any inputs and irrigation. Now, that thatch as cover for houses has almost been wiped-out by durable and lasting plain steel sheets, farmers have replaced their thatch fields ('Khar-bari' in Nepali) with 'amliso' cultivation which gives better economic return.

Growth pattern of broom grass

Broom grass is planted during April and May. The culms arise centrifugally during peak vegetative growth in the month of June and July. It bears inflorescence at the end of vegetative growth. The

15

appearance and growth of culms in a tussock gives a characteristic order that determines the extent of culm growth, size, number, and length of the leaves and the overall shape of the crown. The productive stage starts with the flowering of the plant in the months of October to March. The inflorescence becomes ready for harvest by December and January and the harvest continues until March. The maximum height of a tussock is attained in 3rd year, while basal girth and culms numbers continue to increase.

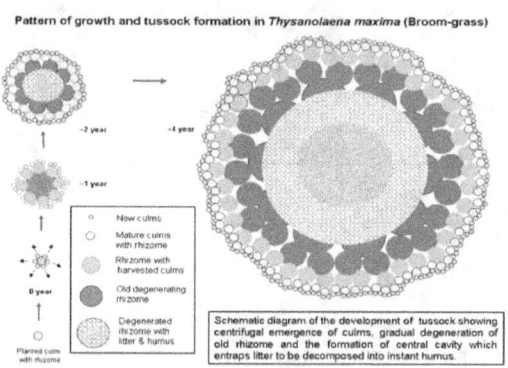

Figure 2.   Growth of tussock year-wise.

Crown structure of broom grass

The number of culms per tussock and basal area of the culms increased simultaneously with age of the plantation, the growth became more vigorous, increased in both inter-nodal length and leaf size. It caused a steady increase in the cumulative leaf area up to 4th year. The number of leaves per Culm remained almost same due to seasonal leaf-fall. The canopy cover increased at a fast rate and reached its maximum at the end of 4th year. The Leaf Area Index (LAI) also increased fast, up to the 3rd year of growth, but lowered down subsequently. The culms laden with leaves and brooms tended to droop down, resulting in maximum canopy cover and moderate LAI in the tussocks of 4th year plantation. The vigour was fairly sustained during the 4th year with a slight decrease, but it significantly decreased beyond the 5th year. The culms grow only toward the periphery in centrifugal order. The resulting central cavity of the tussock remains devoid of any Culm. The growth of the tussocks attained its maximum 3rd year, after which the tussocks showed signs of withering from the inner side and the area of central cavity increased significantly. The culms emerged so closely at the periphery of the cavity that most dead leaf and other biomass remained locked within the cavity. This pattern of growth helps conserving nutrients in the close vicinity of the newly arising culms, which is particularly important in degraded sites prone to soil erosion and also help to improve soil organic matter content.

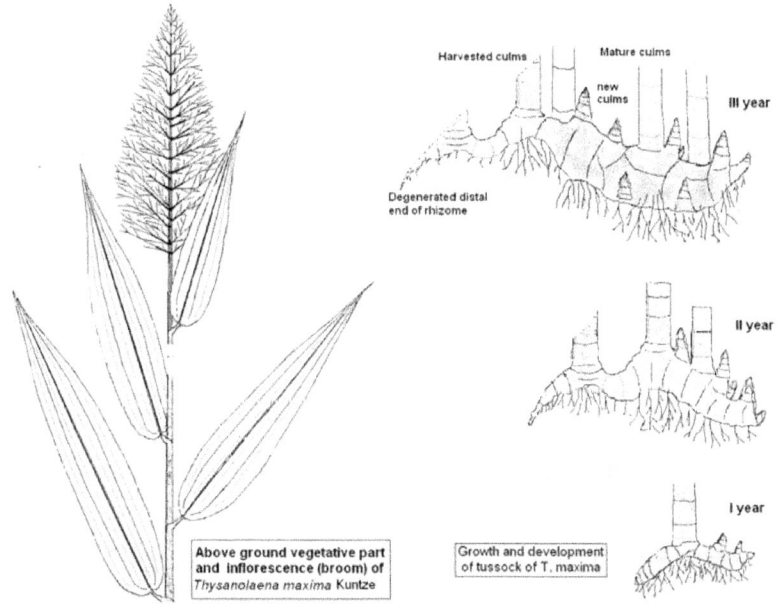

Figure 3.Upper Portion of the culm bearing Panicle (broom) and growth pattern of rhizome (year-wise).

6. Cultivars

Till date, no registered cultivars are available. However, there are two genotypes in Darjeeling Himalaya, 'Kalo Khalay' and 'Seto Khalay', which can be easily identified by the intensity of colour. The 'Kalo Khalay' is dark green and yields more broom and fodder than the 'Seto Khalay'. However, peoples are collecting and transplanting the wild seedlings for propagation but it is always better to get quality seedlings from reputed nurseries.

7. Climate requirements

It is cultivated as rain fed crop in Sikkim, Arunachal Pradesh, Tripura, Darjeeling (West Bengal), Assam and Meghalaya. It tolerates the temperatures ranging from 10-37 ^{0}C. The plant requires a hot moist climate and an elevation between 100 and 2000 m for its cultivation. It can be grown successfully even in areas which receive heavy rainfall with high relative humidity. In its natural habitat, the plant is found growing as shrub.

8. Soil requirement

Broom grass can be cultivated successfully in organic matter rich fertile, well drained forest soils. Red and Laterite soils with high organic matter content and moisture holding capacity are also suitable for cultivation. It is also cultivated on a large scale in limestone soil as in limestone soil and well drained fertile black cotton soil. However light, porous and well-drained soil rich in organic content is most suitable for its cultivation.

Part II: Agro-technological aspects

Cultivation of broom grass

Cultivation of broom-grass is comparatively easy and requires less financial inputs. It can be grown on marginal lands and wastelands. It grows well on a wide range of soils varying from sandy loam to clay loam. The planting can be done by seeds or rhizomes. There is two genotypes in Darjeeling Himalaya, 'Kalo Khalay' and 'Seto Khalay', which can be easily identified by the intensity of colour. The 'Kalo Khalay' is dark green and yields more broom and fodder than the 'Seto Khalay'. However, Some people also collect and transplant the wild seedlings for propagation but it is always better to get quality seedlings from reputed nurseries.

1. Method of Propagation

Tiger grass can be propagated by rhizomes, rooted culms or seeds. It is cultivated mainly for broom making, but not so much for forage. It regenerates through seeds under natural condition. The planting can be done by seeds or rhizomes. Some farmer also collect and transplant the wild seedlings for propagation but it is always better to get quality seedlings from reputed nurseries. The seeds mature during February to March and disseminate by wind to long distances due to their lightweight. Seed dispersal is also affected by water in some areas. The seed germinates in the beginning of the rainy season. The seedling establishment and the growth is good on loose and exposed areas such as landslides and freshly disturbed soil specially near road construction sites where light availability is good.

2. Nursery techniques for Seeds

It can be propagated artificially through seeds, rhizomes and wild seedlings transplant. The seeds are generally available in March after senescing panicles and can be stored in dry condition for 2-3 months. Small mother beds 2m x 1m are prepared and sowing is done by broadcasting 10 to 15 g seeds in each bed. Seeds are covered with very thin layer of sand and the beds with thatch grass. Watering is done as and when required. The germination starts after two to three weeks of sowing. The grass cover is removed on germination of seeds and regular weeding and watering is done. After 5 to 6 weeks the seedlings are either transplanted to other beds at a spacing of 10 cm x 10 cm or in the polythene bags filled with a mixture of soil, sand and farm yard manure in a ratio of 1:2:1. Watering and weeding is done regularly till the seedlings are ready for planting in field in the beginning of next rainy season.

3. Nursery techniques for rooted culms

The rooted culms are collected by digging of roots from wild or cultivated plants after harvesting the crop during February or March. The culms are cut leaving 15-20 cm long stem with roots and used for raising nursery as well as for planting in the field. Two to three culms along with bud sprouts and rhizomes are separated from clump and planted either in poly-bags or in field. The mixture of top soil, sand and farm yard manure in 1:2:1 ratio is used for filling the poly-bags or pits. During transplanting the soil should have sufficient moisture for plant establishment. The plants are watered as and when required and kept in shade. The rhizomes are easy to transport to long distances for propagation as well as for plantation. The cut ends of culms can be dipped in melted wax to prevent drying and decaying. A small clump of rhizome having culms of 4 to 5 nodes is good for planting and almost cent per cent result is obtained by this method. The sprouted rhizomes are ready within three months for transplanting in the field.

4. Preparation of nursery bed

Nursery bed should generally be raised 15-20 cm from ground level and the soil must be fine and have optimum moisture for uniform and high percentage of germination. The length of the bed may be kept 2 to 3 meter and width is restricted to a maximum of 1 meter only to facilitate intercultural operations. Sowing is generally done by broad casting of 5-10 grams seeds in each bed. The beds should preferably be prepared in the east and west direction and line should be made north to south direction on the beds to explore and capture maximum radiation energy.

5. Seed sowing in the nursery

Proper seed sowing in the nursery beds is one of the important factors to get healthy and vigorous seedlings. After the seed bed preparation, seeds are sown in the nursery bed either by broadcasting, although line sowing is the best. About 1 cm deep lines parallel to the width at a distance of 5.0 cm apart are opened and the seeds are sown or placed at a distance of about 1.0-2.0cm in the line. After sowing, the seed bed should be covered with 0.5 cm. thick mixture of farm yard manure: sand: soil in the ratio of 1:1:2 for better moisture conservation and germination. Mulching the seedbeds with dry culms or any mulching material in hot weather with intermittent sprinkling of water and polyethylene mulch helps in quick and uniform germination of seeds. The time to remove the mulch from the seedbed is extremely important. The seedbeds should be observed daily and as and when the white thread like structure is seen above the ground, the mulch should be removed carefully in the evening hours to avoid any damage to the emerging seedlings. During the seedling growth, if temperature reaches above

30^0C then the beds should be covered by green or black coloured 50% or 60% shade nets about 1 meter above the ground with suitable support to protect the seedlings from direct scorching sunlight. The newly introduced translucent blue shade net gives blue light, which is excellent for plant growth. The nursery beds require light irrigation with the help of rose can from the seed sowing until the seedlings become ready to transplant. Young roots of seedlings absorb water primarily by osmotic forces. Anaerobic condition caused by excessive soil moisture retard seed germination. It is important to remove weak, diseased, insect pests damaged and dense plants from the nursery beds keeping 5 to 1.0cm distance from plant to plant for proper growth of the seedlings.

6. Pricking out of seedlings

After 4 to 6 weeks, pricking of seedling is to be done. Pricking out of seedling is a method of producing healthy and hardened seedlings by pricking out the young seedlings when first true leaves have come out and transplanting them to another seed bed or grown individually in small polythene bags. The seedlings should be uprooted carefully with the help of V-notched wooden stick for second transplanting and spaced about 10 cm within a row which are 10 cm apart, both in second seed beds or polythene bags. The soil mixture generally used to grow the pricked out seedlings is slightly richer than the previous one for first seed bed. Watering and weeding is done regularly until the Seedlings become ready for planting in the main field in the beginning of next rainy season.

7. Soil preparation for Main field

Land preparation should be done before or during March and debris are either burnt or removed from the field. The pits of 30 cm³ are dug out one month before the planting and left for weathering. A spacing of 2.5 m x 2.5 m is the best for plain fertile land and 1600 seedlings are required for planting of one hectare area.

While for waste lands or hilly areas planting in contour lines or on the bunds of terraces at a spacing of 1.5 x 2.0 m is good and about 2500 to 3500 plants are required for one hectare area. The farmyard manure and leaf manure at equal proportion per pit are mixed in each pit soil before filling and planting. The spacing may vary with the type of land being used for cultivation. However, good yield can be obtained when it is cultivated on fertile lands.

8. Transplanting

Land preparation should be completed before or during March. It is generally planted at the onset of monsoon during May - June, when soil has sufficient moisture for plant establishment. Several culms sprout from each plant resulting into a clump of culms from every pit.FYM can be applied during the second year also to get better yield. Inflorescence initiation takes place from October onwards.

9. Ratooning

The ratooning can be done up to 6th year of planting. It is better to replant after 6th year of planting. Generally, Maximum yield is obtained from third year onwards. Burning of the fields is necessary after harvesting the crop to boost up the sprouting the new shoots and to obtain high yield from broom grass. The centre of tussock is devoid of new culms during the 4th and 5th year of planting as they arise from the periphery.

10. Fertilization

Nutrient management is a key component for good growth and development of this grass. This prefers to grow where friable soil with rich in humus content. Usually farmer should not apply any nutrient in their field at high altitude range because most of the hilly soils are rich in humas and high organic matter. However at lower elevation (800-1300 m asl) farmer apply roughly FYM and leaf manure.

Our study at Kalimpong (1250 m asl) revealed that vermicompost is very important as because of mixture of worm casts enriched with macro and micronutrients (N, P, K, Mn., Fe, Mo, B, Cu and Zn.), The nutrient level of vermicompost (1-1.5% N, 0.6-0.8% P and 1.2-1.5 K) is higher than any other compost (Table 2). However, farmer can go for other farm household refused to enrich their soil fertility for healthy growth of the plant.

Application of manure

It can be grown without chemical fertilizers and use of organic pesticides, organic manures like farm yard manure (FYM), vermi-compost and green manure etc. may be used as per the need (Table 1). Split application of decomposed manure is preferable. Apply first dose of manue (2/3) before the sowing of transplanted plant

Table 1: Organic inputs recommendation on observation basis at field level.

Input	Quantity required	Remarks (t/ha)
Neem / Pongamiacake	0.50	Protection against termite and other soil borne pest and pathogen.
FYM	10.00	There is possibility of weed infestation and poor establishment of the crop.
Compost	10.00	Possibility of weed and pathogen infestation and poor establishment of the crop.

Vermicompost	0.50	This source is totally weed free and help in better performance of the crop.

Table 2: Average nutrient content of bulky manure which may apply to Broom grass

Manure	Percent Content		
	N_2	P_2O_5	K_2O
1. Animal Refuse:			
Cattle dung, fresh	0.3-0.4	0.1-0.2	0.1-0.3
Night soil, fresh	1.0-1.6	0.8-1.2	0.2-0.6
Poultry manure, fresh	1.0-1.8	1.4-1.8	0.8-0.9
2. Wood Ashes:			
Ash, household	0.5-1.9	1.6-4.2	2.3-12.0
Ash, wood	0.1-0.2	0.8-5.9	1.5-36.0
3. Farm Factory and Habitation:			
Rural compost, dry	0.5-1.0	0.4-0.8	0.8-1.2
Urban compost, dry	0.7-2.0	0.9-3.0	1.0-2.0
FYM, dry	0.4-1.5	0.3-0.9	0.3-1.9
4. Plant Residues:			
Rice hulls	0.3-3.5	0.2-0.5	0.3-0.5
Straw and stalks: Banana, dry	0.61	0.12	1.0

Maize	0.42	1.57	1.65
Paddy	0.36	0.08	0.71
Wheat	0.53	0.10	1.10

11. Irrigation

Actual requirement of irrigation depends upon the climatic conditions. For seed germination field should be irrigated with light sprinkler shower one-two day's interval. Heavy irrigation will misplace the seed and some time due to anaerobic condition for long period leads to poor germination. In main field broom grass need not required any fixed irrigation, however intermittent application two in fortnight is require. Even though broom grass can tolerate dryness, but its growth gets affected when the moisture goes down the optimal level (i.e. field capacity) for the plant. It may be watered intermittently 30 day's interval during November to April. The nursery beds and fields after plantation should be irrigated periodically as and when required weekly or fortnightly. Regular irrigation during lean period may be given a must for proper growth and flowering of plant.

12. Plant Protection

Weeding is required at the early stage of establishment. Attention should be given in the first year of planting, after that, minimum care is required. Cut portion of Rhizome should be dipped in Carbendazim solution@ 0.1g/L to prevent unexpected fungal attack. Broom grasses are susceptible to rodent attacks due to the buildup of nutrients if the undersides are not cleared at least thrice a year.

13. Harvesting

The panicles become tough and its colour turns to light green or red. It can be harvested on maturity during from January to March. Plucking of broom grass panicles may be restricted during December to February for good quality. The harvesting should be done carefully when the brooms have matured properly. The culms are harvested by cutting above the ground, panicles and stem are disjoined. The panicles can also be hand pulled and dried in fields. Harvesting should be done within one week of flowering before pollination to get the best quality of panicles for soft broom. Young and newly sprouted shoots should not be damaged during the harvest. The leaves are harvested for fodder once in the middle of monsoon (August) from second year onwards.

Proper drying of harvested material is essential to ensure quality. Harvested panicle may be loosely laid out in thin layers on top of raised bamboo platforms for drying under the sun and when stock is returned to godown, dew deposition should be avoided to prevent spoiling of the colour and quality of the stock.

14. Yield

The panicles from the grass are harvested from Dec. to March when the panicles become tough and its colour changes to light green or red or brown. Harvesting is done carefully just before maturity without damaging the newly sprouted shoots by cutting above the ground or hand pulled. The panicles are disjointed from culms and dried under direct sunlight for a few days. Burning of the field is necessary to boost up the sprouting of new shoots after harvesting. The yield usually varies from 300 to 500kg of broom material per hectare. The yield differs according to the age of the plantation. The highest yield of inflorescence is obtained from three and four year old plants, which is about 2 kg per plant and then begins to decline, and in the fifth year, the average yield is 1.5

kg, then, in the sixth year, only 0.5 kg of produce per plant is obtained. Yield varies also with genotype, package of practices; the quality of planting materials, spacing, fertility of the land and the cultural practices adopted for maintenance, site selection etc. The ratooning can be done to the 5th year of planting. It is better to replant after 6th year for better economic returns. The yield is low in first and fifth year. The highest yield is obtained in the third year. The maximum growth takes place from 2nd year onwards when annual increment in number of culms per tussock is very high.

15. Agro-economics of cultivation

The estimates for cost of cultivation yield and economic returns of cultivation have been worked out. This information gives a general idea about the economics of cultivation and can be helpful to the farmers and other growers who intends to take up its plantation as a cash crop. it varies according to labour efficiency, wages, soil fertility, cultural practices, market price and demand, etc. The plantation has a rotation of 6 years in which 6 crops are taken annually. Its cultivation can generate approximately ten to twenty thousand rupees in a year from one hectare. The profit can be raised further if brooms are processed by the cultivator themselves. The planting and establishment costs can be saved to great extent if the individual/farmer and his family members take up the works themselves. Broom grass cultivation needs the minimum input of labour and generates a very attractive economic return. it provides a good profit to the growers. The yield varies between 300 and 500kg of broom material per hectare. The yield differs according to the age of the plantation. The highest yield of inflorescence is obtained from three and four year old plants, which is about 2 kg per plant and then begins to decline, and in the fifth year, the average yield is 1.5 kg, then, in the sixth year, only 0.5 kg of produce per plant is obtained. Production costs differ for different years. During the first year, the grower has to invest in small tools, implements, and labour, resulting in the highest production cost. The growers start earning from second year onwards. From one hectare area, the grower can generate an annual profit ranging from Rs. 500 to 11,000 solely from the sale of the inflorescence as brooms. The benefit obtained by the growers varies according to labour efficiency, wages, soil fertility, cultural practices, market price and demand. The benefit- cost ratio calculated at 10, 15, and 20 per cent annual interest rates (AIR) showed that the ratio varied between 3.19 and 3.46. Growers are getting good returns because of low investment and quick production, as it can be harvested annually after one year of planting.

Table 3. Cost-benefit analysis for one-hectare plantation area (Rs.) of broom grass.

	Years						
	1	2	3	4	5	6	Total (Rs.)
Revenue	3,000	5,200	9,570	12,350	4,500	900	35,520
Production Cost	3,700	1,400	1,550	1,550	850	400	9,450
Labour							
1. Site Clearance	1000						1000
2. Weeding (twice/year) & Harvesting (once/year)	1200	1200	1200	1200	650	250	5700
3. Pit Digging and Rhizome Planting	800						800
4. Transportation to Godown	200	200	350	350	200	150	1450
Materials- Small Tools and Implements	500						500
Net Income (Rs.)	-700	3,800	8,020	10,800	3,650	500	26,070

Note: Benefit-cost ratio at 10% annual interest rate (AIR) = 3.46; benefit-cost ratio at 15% AIR = 3.32 Benefit-Cost Ratio at 20% AIR = 3.19. (Source: B.K.Tewari, 2014)

Part III: Post-harvest management aspects

1. Drying and Broom Making

Plucking of broom grass panicles, within one week of flowering and before pollination may be done during December to February for getting best quality raw material for soft broom. Proper drying of harvested panicles is essential to ensure quality. Harvested panicles may be loosely laid out in thin layers on top of raised bamboo platforms for drying under the sun and it is to be re-stored again to avoid dew deposition which can spoil the colour and quality of stock.

Broom Making

For broom making essential materials are 105 panicle (maximum), wooden stick, Tie wire, Plastic string on split rattan. To make one broom, a bundle consisting of 105 panicles (number of panicles may vary depending on the desired thickness of the broom) can be used. Then, Sorting is done of the panicles according to length. Shearing is done some of its first spikelet (panicles) and to ensure an average remaining length is maintained. Then, these sheared panicles are tied to the main stem to add thickness to the broom. Some of the stalks remained to serve as handle. Added panicles are arranged tightly bound with string into five to six small bundles (1-1.5 cm diameter) and banded together to make one big bundle. Then, the stalks are tightly banded together by using tie wire to form the handle. After that, wood or bamboo stick is used as handle. The panicles are banded together and arranged into fan-like form with plastic string or split rattan. Decorate the handle or wrap with rolled plastic or split rattan to indicate the origin of the product. There is no problem in marketing soft brooms as long as these are good in quality. It can be sold within the community where it is produced or anywhere in India.

2. Packaging

After drying of Brooms (panicles) directly can be sold out to whole-seller, without packaging, however, in this case, farmers get minimum price of his product. It is better to sell the product after making broom.

Good packaging of final products, broom, fetches good return to farmers. Though, There is no problem in marketing soft brooms as long as these are good in quality. It can be sold within the community where it is produced or anywhere in India.

3. Storage

As it is season based, high volume crop, it needs storage facilities to get faire price. Broom grass cultivation has a high benefit-cost ratio and it has a very good market. Even without much intervention, farmers can fetch good returns because of low investment and quick production, as it can be harvested annually after one year of planting.

4. Marketing

It has sufficient demand throughout the country and marketing is not a problem as Brooms are required in each household. The majority of the production is from subsistence farming areas and dispersed collection from the forest, which are inaccessible to transport networks and markets. It is a high volume crop and there is glut in the market during the harvesting season which reduces the local price. Whole sale trading of brooms is a highly monopolized. Major portion of income goes to the traders and middlemen. The farmer gets very meager amount i.e., about 30-35% of the retailers'- price. Therefore, to improve the economy of people and region, the system of cooperative marketing needs to be developed.

Part IV: Calendar of operation

CALENDER OF OPERATION FOR NURSERY	
1. March-April :	Selection of site for sucker nursery, cleaning the site, opening the pit/trench.
2. May-June :	Filling the pit/trench with top soil, FYM, Compost and planting of suckers, staking and mulching.
3. July :	Planting of suckers may be continued.
4. August :	Monitoring the nurseries.
5. September-October:	Weeding and application of organic manures.
6. November-December to protects	Erection of shades in high altitudes suckers from low temperature and frost.
7. January-Febuary	Mulching and irrigation.

Month	Activities (crop calendar for Main field)
December-January	Provide shade in nurseries at higher altitude to reduce damage due to low temperature/frost. Panicles can be collected from the previous season planted suckers.
Febuary-March	Filling the pit/trench with top soil, FYM, Compost and planting of suckers, staking and mulching. Monitor the plantation for incidence of rodents in the nurseries irrigation may be given.
April-May	Monitor the plantation.
June –July	New suckers can be planted from nursery to main fields.
August	Monitor the plantation.
September-October	Harvesting in the low and mid altitude. Follow the phyto-sanitary measures.
November-December	Harvesting in the high altitude. Follow the Phytosanitary measures.

Part V: Problems of Shifting Cultivation

1. As shifting cultivation is done in steep hill-sides, it leads to increase in soil erosion and land-slides.

2. For land preparation in hilly tract takes more labour for planting crops as it is difficult to plough.

3. It is more difficult to irrigate the crops as per need.

4. Nutrient content in soil is low in the steep hill-sides.

5. Slash and burn agriculture create negative impact to biodiversity.

Part VI: Utilization aspects

Advantages of Broom grass Cultivation

Broom grass may play vital role to promote rural livelihood for improving the socio-economic condition. It's cultivation more profitable site specific; selection of a suitable superior genotype /variety is very important for ecological and economic benefits. The production of quality planting stock for specific uses will help in development of this cash crop.

1. Source of Income

Broom cultivation is economically viable. It requires low inputs and management and gives high return. Farmers may able to get 1st year i.e. same year as planted (when planting in May-June and Harvesting in November-December) one broom from 3-4 bushes which may fetch 1 dollar. Depending upon the shape and method of making, one broom may take about 300-400 grams of broom grass flowers. Value addition to raw-material broom like broom making and the farmers make brooms that are of good design fetch gives extra income to farmer. Farmers can earn by selling broom grass sapling to other fellow farmers. The trade of broom grass cultivation benefits almost all sections of society, as the landowners benefit from broom cultivation, the landless benefit by daily wage labour and the traders and the transporters earn their livelihood by marketing the broom. Cultivation of broom grass is gradually becoming popular in Darjeeling Himalaya, particularly among the marginal and subsistence farmers. The farmers are getting good returns as investment is low and production is quick, without any external intervention, as broom grass may begin to be harvested one year after planting compare to large cardamom, which is major cash crop.

2. Prevents Soil erosion and Bioengineering potentiality

Engineering functions of broom grasses are catch, armor, reinforce, anchor, support and drain (Clark and Hellin, 1996).Broom grasses that spread in clumps and have multitudinous tangled up roots are more effective in preventing the surface soil erosion in steep hillsides with sandy loam soil as its root spread out to at least one meter below the ground. The leaves and root decrease the speed of the rain water drops, absorb water from soil and reduces the speed of flowing water after heavy rain, thus, effectively reducing the chances of surface soil erosion. It has phyto-remediation potential in waste water treatment and stabilization of mined out areas and can be planted in degraded soils where other plants do not grow (Nicholson *et. al.,*2008). Broom grass has excellent capacity to catch, moderately useful armor, excellent reinforce and moderately useful support. The fibrous root- mat effectively protects the top soil and nutrients from erosion sloping terrain, landslides affected areas and agricultural fields. Water run-off and soil loss reduced by up to 88% as compared to bare local (Bhucher, 2002). It grows in a wide range of habits with soil PH ranging from 5.3-9.3, moisture from 11.6-37.6%, organic carbon from 0.4 2.7% and nitrogen from 0.007-0.31% (Palni *et. al.,* 1999; Bhuchar, 2002). Contour planting with tiger grass shows better performance in terms of vegetative cover, surface runoff and erosion yield in newly burned pine watershed; cheapest among the treatments investigated for re-vegetation and rehabilitation. It is suitable hedge-row species in controlling soil loss (55-80%) and runoff (30-70%) using CHIAT (Khisa, 2001).Broom grass has excellent hydrologic functions of soil binding capacity and ground surface protection, interception, storage, leaf drip but moderate infiltration (Kafle, 2005).Improves soil fertility and productivity when planted with *Cajanus cajan* than as a sole crop (RFRI, 2007). Improves forage production and soil conservation if planted in agriculture terrace margins without affecting the productivity of the crops. Effective vegetative barrier in controlling

37

soil erosion, improving crop yield and restoring soil fertility (although not as comparable with the other two grasses studied) (Sudhishri *et. al.,* 2008).

Table 4: Impacts of different crops on potentiality on Bio-engineering of broom grass.

Plot Type	Water runoff	Soil Loss	Conservation value (water)	Conservation value (soil)
	(liter)	(kg)	(%)	(%)
Maize	25±4	1.51±0.16	69	56
Finger-mullet	18±3	1.32±0.14	78	62
Mixed cropping	12±3	0.95±0.12	85	73
Large cardamom	15±3	0.45±0.06	81	87
Broom grass	10±2	0.41±0.07	88	88
Bare land	80±11	3.46±0.35	-	-

(Source : Kafle, 2005)

Land Use Type	Soil loss (t/yr/ha)	Runoff (%)
Outward sloping terrace	10.4	2.8
Degraded land	21.3	40.1
Degraded land treated with broom grass	12.6	16.5

(Source : Kafle, 2005)

Table 5: Bioengineering Characteristics of broom grass.

Rooting depth	Quantity of planting material required
7.0 to 9.5 m	For single row of 5m, 10m, 25m, 50m, 75m, 100m length, quantity of planting material is 4, 10, 21, 31 and 41 respectively.
Root lateral spread 10.3 to 13.2 m radial	For double row of 5m, 10m, 25m, 50m, 75m, 100m length, quantity of planting material is 5, 11, 29, 62, 92 and 122 respectively
Height 3.2 to 4.9 m	Shade effect Max. 6.8m for mean height 3.9m
Ground surface area protected by foliage against direct raindrop effect	Type of root Fibrous
47.19 to 82.87 m2	

Mean: 66.49 m2	
Volume of Soil bound by roots 2.33 to 5.20 m3	Propagation Slip cuttings
Mean: 3.78 m3	
Effective Spacing :Plain: 2.40 m , Slope: 1.80 m	

(Source : Kafle, 2005)

Pictorial presentation of Bio-engineering of broom grass

3. Fodder for livestock

It is difficult to get green grass for livestock during dry season but broom grass can provide fresh green fodder. Young, tender culms, leaves and tips are used as fodders for cattle, buffaloes and rabbits. One of the most preferred fodders for butterfat production among ruminants; palatable to livestock even during rain or cold weather conditions. It satisfies appetite of buffalo for 6.33 hrs. Rumen degradability after 48 h ranges within 404 to 488 g/kg. It can help not only in increasing milk production, also effective in cleaning

40

animal stomach. The leaves have balanced proportion of nutrients qualifying them as good forage and fodder for livestock.

Table 5: Nutritional Values of Leaf of broom grass

Parameters	Palni *et al.* (1995)	Singh *et al.* (1996)	Bhuchar (2002)
Digestibility	57.9	-	54.3 - 57.9
Total Ash	11.8	5.65	10.7
Ether extract	6.67	1.94	4.2 - 6.7
N-free extract	33.1	51.6	39.3
Crude protein	18.1	10.2	15.1
Crude fiber	30.4	30.5	29.5 - 31.0
Cellulose	30.2	-	30.3 - 37.8
Hemicellulose	29.6	-	29.6
Lignin	9.1	-	4.6

(Source: Bhuchar, 2008)

However, some worker highlights the draw-back of broom grass as fodder. It produces more foliage (Kafle, 2005), however, its leaf to stem ratio is less. Palatability is less; causes haematuria among cattle and buffaloes (Joshi & Singh, 1989). It is preferred fodder for milk production, but animal response is low.

4. Fire wood and furniture from the stalk

After harvesting of panicles and young tender branches to feed livestock, the remaining matured stalks can be used for firewood and fencing. Matured stalks can also be used to prepare book self and other furniture.

5. Conservation of Biodiversity and environment

Commercial cultivation of broom grass helps to ignite the biodiversity and environmental conservation as it is evergreen plant. It has contributed to protecting other species by allowing them regrowing. Its cultivation promotes nature friendly, cost-effective and sustainable use of fragile and degraded lands. Roots bind the soil and protect topsoil and nutrient erosion on sloping terrain, agricultural fields and landslide. It can be used as backup fodder grass on contour strips and terrace risers, a good soil cover, a crop to maximize land use, a tool for management of hill ecosystem, a protection from forest fires and a slope stabilizer in steep land of hills. As It is C4 species; can withstand drought (Saxena and Ramakrishnan, 1983).Villagers (65%) in Nepal reported that broom grass is the best adapted species for climate change(Khadka, 2011).Significant rise (83%) in broom grass cultivation in Meghalaya, India during the past three decades because it is least affected by climate change (Lyngdoh & Baishya, 2010).

6. Medicinal uses

The extract from the root suckers is used to check boils. Pills prepared from the leaves are taken twice daily for the treatment of tuberculosis. In case of retention of placenta in cows, the plant is fed for easy and immediate release. Leaf extract exhibited moderate attractive potency to oriental fruit fly, a destructive pest. Juice of young stem is used to treat red and dirty eyes. Roots applied in worm diseases of cattle. Whole plant is used to treat hypo-tensive and spasmo-lytic, leaf paste of *Litsea lancifolia* mixed with leaf paste of *Thysanolaena maxima* is given to dysentery. Seeds powdered are given to women before child birth to facilitate delivery; the flour is used as abortifacient and contraceptive. When the navel cord of a newly-born child has to be cut, the leaf is used as a knife without any infection. The leaves of broom grass have a balanced proportion of nutrients showed a positive balance for calcium, phosphorous and nitrogen (Palni *et al.,* 1999).The root paste is believed to cause abortion. The decoction of its roots is used as a mouth-wash during fever and paste of dried of fresh roots applied on the skin to check the boils (Rai and Sharma, 1994).Root decoction is used to treat mumps, ulcers, abscesses and paste applied to carbuncles. Its root has antihelmentic, anti-microbial properties (Mahato and choudhury, 2005).Root used in flatulence (Jana and Chouhan, 2000), flowers in rheumatic pain and skin swelling (Maity *et al.,* 2004).

7. **Ornamental, hedge crop and others uses**

The grass is occasionally planted for ornamental purposes and as a hedge. It can be used for landscape and ornamental purposes (Ramm Botanicals, 2009), dyed panicles in carnival customs and decorative extenders (Fetalvero *et al.,* 2011), Grass can be used as weed suppressor (Kisa *et al.,* 1999), roofing material, wrapper for steamed foods; substrate for the cultivation of oyster mushroom (Srijumpa, 2002). Leaves have been tried in cellulase and ethanol production (Yimyong *et al.,* 2005). It is a potential source of raw material for pulp-and- paper making industries either alone or in combination with other raw materials (Saikia *et al.,* 1992). Fibers (1.25 mm long) are obtained from the culms at 45% yield and are processed into papers. Paper properties are Burst factor: 30; Breaking length: 3,555; Tear factor: 106.It has the comparative advantage of tolerance to harsh environmental conditions such as steep rocky mountain slopes, shallow soil, drought and high rainfall conditions. Therefore, it is suitable to grow on wastelands, jhum fallow, as well as in homesteads. After the harvest, the broom sticks (stem) are used as wall building material in Assam and other parts of this region. The sticks have also been tried by paper and pulp industries for the manufacture of paper. Pulps are processed into insulation boards with very good strength but moderate heat insulating properties. Moisture resistance compared favorably with the imported ones(Razzaque and Khan, 1978).The cultivation of this grass can wean away the practice of shifting cultivation and reduce the dependence of people on forests. It has phyto-remediation potential in waste water treatment and stabilization of mined out areas and can be planted in degraded soils where other plants do not grow (Nicholson et al., 2008).Broom grass is comparable with vetiver grass (*Vetiver zizaimoides*) for phyto-stabilization. It shows very high tolerance to lead concentrations in its roots and shoots up to 100,000mg/kg. Application of inorganic fertilizer (150mg/kg) improves its growth and uptake of Lead (Pb) while amending the soil with pig manure reduces the roots' uptake and transport of Lead (Pb) (Rotkittikhun, *et. al.*, 2007). Pot and field experiments were conducted to elucidate the phytostabilization potential of two grass species (*Thysanolaena maxima* and *Vetiveria zizanioides*) with respect to lead (Pb) tailing soil. Three fertilizers (Osmocote® fertilizer, cow manure, and organic fertilizer) were used to improve the physicochemical properties of tailing soil. *V. zizanioides* treated with organic fertilizer and cow manure showed the highest biomass $(14.0 \pm 2.6$ and 10.5 ± 2.6 g per plant, respectively) and the highest Pb uptake in the organic fertilizer treatment (*T. maxima*, 413.3 µg per plant; *V. zizanioides*, 519.5 µg per plant) in the pot study, whereas in field trials, *T. maxima* attained the best performances of dry biomass production $(217.0 \pm 57.9$ g per plant) and Pb uptake (32.1 mg per plant) in the Osmocote® treatment. In addition, both grasses showed low translocation factor (<1) values and bioconcentration coefficients for root (>1). During a 1-year field trial, T. maxima also produced the longest shoot $(103.9 \pm 29.7$ cm), followed by *V. zizanioides* $(70.6 \pm 16.8$ cm), in Osmocote® treatment. Both grass species showed potential as excluder plants suitable for phytostabilization applications in Pb-contaminated areas (Meeinkuirt *et.al.* 2013).

There is a ample scientific evidence supporting the potential and significance of broom grass as a multi-purpose crop. The grass is best adapted for climate change due to its C4 nature and based from reports from the field about its tolerance to drought plus the increasing number of farms established each year. It can be an environment-friendly alternative in restoring mined out areas in the country as it was found to absorb lead and antimony. It can help mitigate climate-change related disasters because of its water and soil conservation and bioengineering potential. Its potential as a traditional herbal remedy must be scientifically validated and its potential as feeds must be perfected. Its potential as feedstock for biomass technologies must be explored through Private Partnership model.

Part VII: Challenges to commercial broom cultivation

The best way to ensure the continuous supply of best quality broom can be done by domestication through adopting correct agro-techniques to produce quality raw material. However, n-number of lacking creating a huge gap to popularizing brooms cultivation. These are as follows:

1. Good Agricultural Practices (**GAP**) and Good Agricultural Collection Practices (**GACP**) for broom grass not yet developed.

2. **Standardize agro-technology** yet to be work out for region and altitude specific for cultivation of broom.

3. **Capacity to outcompete native species**

   Extensive survey should be carried out to identify best superior clone which can compete the foreign one in all the parameters viz., length of inflorescence, total number of shoots, number of new shoots and growth of tussock. During the survey genetic diversity and variations needs to be observed the colour and size of the inflorescence and number of culms per tussock, which are the main economic part of the plant to find out best clone. Promising clone can be multiplied and distributed to the local growers for planting.

4. **It is susceptible to fire, needs to be taken care.**

5. **Variety for broom grass is not yet developed for cultivation.**

   Genetic improvement is aimed at improving the yield and quality of broom-grass for making it suitable for cultivation and to provide higher economic return. Selection of desirable and superior genotypes is the key of all applied genetic improvement programmes. The objective is to obtain sufficient amount of genetic gain as quickly and inexpensively as possible. All the methods of selection are based on general principle of choosing most desirable individuals for use as parents in breeding and production programmes. The parameters for genetic improvement should be (i) sprouting ability of clones or number of culms (tillers) per clump, length of panicle or brooms, (ii) height and growth of clumps, toughness of rachis and softness of ultimate floral branches, (v) number of floral branches per inflorescence, and disease and pest resistance. The literature on this species is scanty and no scientific study had been made so far on intra-specific variations, genetic improvement, developing cultivars and cultivation practice etc.

6. **Overconsumption makes it vulnerable to local extinction.**

Broom grass grows luxuriantly in all the North Eastern States. However, as on date, there is no record of any farmer in the state having taken up commercial cultivation of this multipurpose grass. The green leaves when properly harvested can be used as fodder. After removing the inflorescences/ sticks (Broom), the woody stem (culms) can be used for fuel, fencing, pulp for paper making or other purpose which gives an additional income but still remains unattended in promoting cultivation. Due to unscientific harvesting and over exploitation such unlimited plant bio-resources or natural genetic stock, that could be converted into immediate cash and be used in sustainable manners, is going to be extinct.

7. **Depletion of gene pool of broom grass.**

The natural gene pool of broom grass is depleting rapidly mainly due to biotic pressure and developmental activities. The major causes are seedling mortality due to browsing and grazing, depletion of seed bank and conversion of forest lands for cultivation and construction purposes etc. Large-scale collection of panicles before senescence and dispersal of seeds from brooms impoverishes the soil seed bank.To conserve the depleting gene pool of the different species, field gene banks needs to be established at different places region-wise, altitude-wise for enriching the gene diversity field gene bank. Demonstration farm of broom-grass needs to be established for creating awareness through demonstration and training programmes for the local people.

Part VIII: Present Status of Broom Grass Research and Future Scope

Least efforts have been given to this valuable crop for domestication. Literature on broom grass cultivation is scanty. Information on Superior genotype, intra- specific variation, genetic improvement, development of region-specific cultivars, Good agricultural practice, Agro-economic is not available. By considering potential for improving the livelihood of rural poor in entire Northeast Region including Darjeeling and Sikkim, systematic scientific studies should be worked out. Field gene bank needs to be established for conservation of genetic diversity in multi-location. Altitude specific superior genotype should be identified. The efforts should be given on genetic improvement and development of suitable cultivation technique should be developed for proper domestication of this multipurpose crop.

Present Status of Broom Grass Research

Role in climate change of broom grass

It is the best adapted species for climate change due its fibrous roots (Khadka, 2011). Due to higher efficiency in nutrient uptake of broom grass and low nutrient demand per unit dry matter production and ability to convert significantly greater proportions of dry matter as well as nutrients to below ground tissues make it a highly drought resistant species (Saxena and Ramakrishnan, 1983).There has been significant rise (83%) in broom grass cultivation during the past three decades and a large portion of land is used for this purpose because these grasses fetched the villagers

48

a better price (Lyngdoh and Baishya,2010).

Phytoremedy Potentiality of broom grass

Broom grass has the phyto-remediation potential in waste water treatment and stabilization of mined out areas. Tiger grass can be planted in degraded soils where other plants do not grow (Nicholson *et. al.,* 2008).

Soil conservation Potentiality of broom grass

It was noticed that broom grass can be effectively used in bio-engineering as an effective and low cost measure. It was found out that plots treated with broom grass can reduce water runoff and soil loss by up to 88% as compared to bare land. It was evaluated that the performance of broom grass along with four other grasses as a bioengineering device. It was found that it has an excellent catch, moderately useful armor, excellent reinforce and moderately useful support. Effective spacing of Broom grass for bioengineering purposes is 2.4 m in plain and 1.8 m in slope with maximum effective rooting depth of 0.5 to 1 m. Its root binds up to 5.19 m^Jsoil (Kafle, 2005). It substantially reduces water runoff and soil loss from degraded land. Conservation Value (CV) of 53.1 % and 58.0% were recorded for water runoff and soil loss, respectively (Bhuchar, 2001).Effect of stone bunds and vegetative barriers like Broom grass; *Vetiveria zizanioides* and *Saccharum* spp. on erosion, crop yield and soil properties in degraded hill slopes was studied in Eastern India. Broom was found to be an effective vegetative barrier in controlling soil erosion, improving crop yield and restoring soil fertility (Sudhishri *et. al.,* 2008).

Economic feasibility in Agro-forestry System of broom grass

Broom grass can be adapted to as inter-crop in agro-forestry systems. By doing so, the rural communities can be able to improve

49

the overall ecological condition and benefit economically by setting up a broom industry at individual and/or community level; alternatively the foliage can be used as a good fodder. A potential model has been developed under agri-horticultural based broom grass, which is much suitable in Hill track of Northeast India. Studies have been undertaken on intercropping and it has been seen that soil fertility and productivity are better when broom grass was planted with perennial arahar (*cajanus cajan*) as sole crop (ICFRE, 2008). It can be used in Contour-Hedgerow Intercropping Agroforestry Technology (CHIAT) a farming technology used in reducing soil erosion and improving soil fertility (Khisa, 2001).It's cultivation on agriculture terrace margins improves forage production and soil conservation without affecting the productivity of the crops. It was reported that 1 kg of fresh rhizome planted at a distance of 1 m x 1 m yielded about 16 ton/ha of aboveground biomass in the third year of plantation (Bhuchar, 2008).

Ecological aspects of broom grass:

It is a multipurpose, perennial grass of high fodder value was studied by Bhuchar (2001).It was found that it grows in a wide range of habitats (soil pH: 5.3-9.3; moisture: 11.6-37.6%; carbon: 0.4-2.7%). Its maximum growth is recorded during September. The rhizome is formed during winter season; it is susceptible to long duration of frost. It can be propagated through use of cut rhizomes during winter and early summer months (May).The biomass of rhizome/ slip propagated clumps is maximum during the 3rd year and declined. chlorophyll fluorescence was affected by low temperature; the photosynthetic efficiency of the plants was more during the winter season when they were kept inside a polypit; at ambient and elevated CO_2 concentrations, the rate of photosynthesis of both seedlings and mature clumps increased with increasing PPFD up to 2000 PAR (when other conditions were favorable). At elevated CO_2net photosynthesis was higher than that at ambient concentration. At 330 μ mol mol^1 CO_2 maximum photosynthesis was observed at 25°C, as compared to 30°C for 700Mmol mol^1 CO_2concentration.

Future research Scope of broom grass

Due to unscientific and over harvesting of broom grass panicle, before pollination lead to extinction of species populations (Shankar, *et. al.,* 2001; Pandit *et. al.,* 2008). Excessive harvests also lead to the loss of genetic diversity in the species in natural stock. It has been observed that the productivity decrease after 4 years. It is susceptible to rodent attacks particularly if the undersides are not cleared at least thrice a year (Fetalvero *et. al.,* 2011). Studies should be carried out to deal with the problem so that the productivity doesn't decrease during the fourth year and subsequent years. Studies should be concentric to overcome challenges.

Part IX: Conclusion

The broom grass can play vital role for improving the rural livelihood of entire hill track of north-eastern India. It has potential use in soil conservation, herbal medicine, phyto-remediation and climate change adaptation. Due to biotic pressure and developmental activities are leading to depletion of its genetic resources in natural stock. Superior genotype, intra- specific variation, genetic improvement, development of region-specific cultivars, Good agricultural practice, Agro-economic needs to be worked out for popularizing broom grass. Domestication of the species can contribute to economic growth and improve ecological needs of the communities. This will in turn help in conserving the species diversity and gene pool of the species. However, the major constraints in this practice are identified as inadequate credit and storage facilities to the collectors and growers. They often suffer due to low price paid to them by the local traders. Proper post harvest management with processing and value addition facilities needs to be standardized for enhancing the economic growth of broom grass cultivators. Cultivation of broom grass should be done in waste lands which remain barren/fellow in the hill track for multipurpose use. Hand on Training on cultivation, management practices, proper harvesting, drying and storage of broom grass can be conducted for creating awareness among the farming community. Training on broom making and packaging can be conducted for encouraging the rural entrepreneurship.

References

Arnold, J.E.M. and Ruiz Perez, M. (1998).The role of non-timber forest products in conservation and development. In: Wollenberg E, Ingles A, editors. Income from the forests. Methods for the development and conservation of forest products for local communities. Bogor (Indonesia): CIFOR. p.17– 41.

Arnold,JEM, and Ruiz Perez M. (2001). Can non-timber forest products match tropical conservation and development objectives? *Ecol Econ*. 39:437–447.

Barua, K.N., Bora, I.K., and Baruah, A.(2011). Sustainable management of degraded jhum fallow through plantation of *Thysanolaena maxima* (Roxb.) O. Kuntze (broom grass) in different spacing trial. *Ecobios*., 4 (1 & 2): 31-37

Bell, MJ., and. Garside, AL. (2005). Shoot and stalk dynamics and the yield of sugarcane crops in tropical and subtropical Queensland, Australia. *Field Crops Res*; 92: 231-248

Bhuchar, S. (2008). Broom grass: A multipurpose plant with erosion control potential. *HMCAT Newsletter*, pp. 16-18.

Bhuchar, S. K. (2001). An eco-physiological evaluation of *Thysanolaena maxima* (broom grass): a multipurpose, perennial grass of high fodder value. Ph. D. Thesis submitted to Kumaun University, Nainital, India. 171 p.

Bisht N. S. and Ahlawat S. P. (1998). Broom Crass. SFRI *Technical Bulletin* No. 6. State Forest Research Institute, Itanagar. Arunachal Pradesh.

Charman, P.E.V. and Murphy, B.W.(1992).A soil conservation handbook for New South Wales. Sydney: Sydney University Press.

Chopra, K. (1993). The value of non-timber forest products: An estimation for tropical deciduous forests in India. *Econ Bot.* 47:251 – 257.

Fetalvero, E. G.(2012). Tiger grass, *Thysanolaena maxima* (Roxb.) O. Kuntze: a review of its biology and uses. Retrieved 6th May 2016 from http://www.scribd.com/doc/105368991/Tiger-Grass-Thysanolaena-Maxima-Review-of-Its-Biology-and-Uses.

Fetalvero, E. G., Faminial, T. F. and Sespefie, J.S.(2011). Tiger grass industry in Marigondon Norte, San Andres, Romblon : Implications for research and development. *Travesia*, 1(1):81- 95.

Gangwar A. K, Ramakrishnan PS. (1990). Ethnobiological notes on some tribes of Arunachal Pradesh, northeastern India. *Econ Bot.* 44:94 – 105.

Haridasan, K. and Rao, R.R. (1985 – 1987). Forest flora of Meghalaya. Volumes I and II. Dehra Run (India): Bishen Singh and Mahendra Pal Singh.

Henkemans, A.B. (2001). Tranquilidad and hardship in the forest livelihoods and perceptions of Camba forest dwellers in the northern Bolivian Amazon [dissertation]. Utrecht (The Netherlands): Utrecht University.

Hooker, J.D. 1854. *Himalayan journals*. 2 vols. London (UK): John Murray.

ICFRE, (2008). Improvement of degraded shifting cultivation through the introduction of *Thysanolaena maxima* along with Cajanus cajan as N, fixing plant. In: *Annual Report* 2007-2008 (p. 16 pages). Rain Forest Research Institute, Jorhat.

Jana, S. K. and Chauhan, A. S. (2000).Ethnobotanical studies on Lepchas of Dzongu, North Sikkim. *Ann For*, 8(1):131.

Joshi, N.B. and Singh, S.B.(1989). Availability and use of shrubs and tree fodders in Nepal. Proc. shrubs and Tree fodders for Farm aninamls,IDRC,e.p.211-220

Kafle, C. (2005). Evaluation of effectiveness of root and foliage system of grasses used in soil conservation. Kathmandu, Nepal: Unpublished Thesis at Tribhuvan University.

Khadka, C. (2011). Impacts of climate change on production of cash crops in Annapurna Conservation Area: A case study from LwangChalel Village Development Committee, Kaski District. Kathmandu, Nepal: Unpublished Thesis at Tribhuvan University.

Khisa, K. (2001). Contour hedgerow inter-cropping agroforestry technology for degraded hillside farms at Chittagong Hill Tracts. National Workshop on Agroforestry Research (pp. 179- 184). Khagrachari: Chittagong Hill Tracts Development Board.

Khisa, S. K., Alam, M. K. and Siddiqi, N. A.(1999). Broom grass (*Thysanolaena maxima*) hedges: a bioengineering device for soil erosion control and slope stabilization. First Asia-Pacific Conference on Ground and Water Bioengineering for Soil Erosion Control and Slope Stabilization, (pp. 143-149). Manila.

Kumar, R., Sood, S., Sharma, S., Kasana, RC., Pathania, VL., Singh, B. and Singh, RD. 2014. Effect of plant spacing and organic mulch on growth, yield and quality of natural sweetener plant Stevia and soil fertility in western Himalayas. *Int. J of Plant Pro.,* 8(3): 311-334

Lachungpa, C. (1998). A perspective planning of river valley project in Tista catchment. Pp. 683-688 in Rai, S. C., Sundriyal. R. C. & Sharma, E. (Eds.) Sikkim —Perspectives for Planning and Development. Sikkim Science Society, Tadong, Sikkim, India

Lyngdoh, E. K. and Baishya, R. (2010). People's perception on climate change: A case study from Meghalaya. New Delhi, India:LEAD India.

Mahato, R. B. and Chaudhary R. P. (2005). Ethnomedicinal study and antibacterial activities of selected plants of Palpa District, Nepal. *Scientific World*, 3(3):26-31.

Maity, D., Pradhan, N., and Chauhan, A. J. (2004). Folk uses of some medicinal plants from North Sikkim. *Indian Journal of Traditional Knowledge,* 3 (1):66-71.

Mallik, R.H. 2000. Sustainable management of non-timber forest products in Orissa: Some issues and options. *Indian J Agri Econ.* 55:384 – 397.

Mathema, P. and Singh, B. K. (2003) Soil Erosion Studies in Nepal: Results and Implications. Kathmandu: Department of Soil Conservation and Watershed Management.

Meeinkuirt,W.,Kruatrachue,M.Tanhan,P.,Chaiyarat,R.,Pokethitiyook ,P.(2013).Phytostabilization Potential of Pb Mine Tailings by Two Grass Species,*Thysanolaena maxima* and *Vetiveria zizanioides. Water, Air, & Soil Pollution.* 224:1750

Mosavia, S.G.R., Seghatoleslamia, M.J., Javadib, H. and Ansari-Niab, E. (2009). Effect of plant density and planting pattern on yield, yield components and morphological traits of forage sorghum in second cultivation. *Plant Ecophysiology,* 2;81-84

Neumann , R.P. and Hirsch ,E. (2000). Commercialization of non-timber forest products: Review and analysis of research. Bogor (Indonesia): CIFOR.

NHD (National Human Development Report). 2002. Planning commission, government of India. Available from: http://www.igidr.ac.in/conf/ysp/nhd2001.pdf.

Nicholson, K., Ketphanh, S. and Sengdala, K. (2008). Mission Report: Review of Experience in the Marketing, production, Harvesting and Management of Agro-biodiversity and NTFP products for the agro-biodiversity initiative.

Pandit, B. H., Albano, A. and Kumar, C. (2008). Improving forest benefits for the poor: Learning from community-based forest enterprises in Nepal. Bogor, Indonesia: Center for international Forestry Research.

Pascoe, E.H. (1950). A manual of the geology of India and Burma. Vol 1. 3rd Ed. Calcutta (India): Government of India Press.

Pilani,L.,M.S.,Kothyari,B.P.,Rikhari,H.C.,Buchar,S.,Negi,G.C.S.,Sharma,E.,Samant,S.S.,Bisth,S. and Choudhury,D. (1994). *Thyasanolaena maxima* (Roxb.) Kutnze: a multipurpose,perennial grass of high fodder value. *Hima-Paryavaran* 6 (1): 9

Rai, L.C. and Sharma, A.E. (1994). Medicinal Plants of the Sikkim Himalaya-Status, Use and Potential Himavikas Occasional Publication No. 5. G. B. Pant Institute of Himalayan Environment and Development, Almora, India, 152

Rai, M. B. (2003). Medicinal plants of Tehrathum District, Eastern Nepal. *Our Nature,* 1:42-48.

Ramakrishnan, P.S. (1985). Conservation of rainforests in northeastern India. In: Singh JS, editor. Environmental regeneration in the Himalaya: Concepts and strategies. Nainital (India): *Central Himalayan Environment Association.* p. 69 – 84.

Ramm Botanicals. (2009). Colours of paradise. Ramm Botanicals: http://www.ramm.com.au

Rao, P, Barik, S.K, Pandey, H.N. and Tripathi, R.S. (1990). Community composition and tree population structure in a subtropical broadleaved forest along a disturbance gradient. *Vegetat.* 88:151 – 162.

Razzaque, M.A. and Khan, M.S. (1978). Insulation boards from five grass species of the Chittagong region in Bangladesh. *Bano Biggyan Patrika,* 7 (1-2): 30-37.

Ros-Tonen, M.A.F. and Wiersum, K.F. (2003). The importance of non timber forest products for forest based rural livelihoods: An evolving research agenda. Paper presented at the GTZ/CIFOR International Conference on Livelihoods and Biodiversity, Bonn, Germany.

Ros-Tonen ,M.A.F. (2000). The role of non-timber forest products in sustainable tropical forest management. *Holz als Roh-und Werkstoff.* 58:196 – 201.

Rotkittikhun, P., Chaiyarat, R., Kruatrachue, M., Pokethitiyook,P., and Baker, A. J. M. (2007). Growth and lead accumulation by the grasses *Vetiveria zizanioides* and *Thysanolaena maxima* in lead-contaminated soil amended with pig manure and fertilizer: a glasshouse study. Chemosphere, 66:45–53.

Rotkittikhun, P., Kruatrachue, M., Chaiyarat, R., Ngernsansaruay,C., Pokethitiyook, P., and Paijitprapaporn, A., (2006). Up-take and accumulation of lead by plants from the Bo Ngamlead mine area in Thailand. Environmental Pollution, 144:681–688.

Saikia,D.C., Goswami,T. and Chaliha, B.P.(1992). Paper from *Thysanolaena maxima. Bioresource Technology* 40(3):245-248 .DOI: 10.1016/0960-8524(92)90150-V

Saxena, K.G. and Ramakrishnan, P.S. (1983). Growth and allocation strategies of some perennial weeds of slash and burn agriculture (jhum) in north eastern India. *Canadian Journal of Botany,* 61 (4): 1300-1306.

Shakleton, S.E. and Campbell, B.M. 2007. The traditional broom trade in Bushbuckridge, South Africa: Helping poor women cope with adversity. *Econ Bot.* 61:256 – 268.

Shankar, U., Lama, S.D., Bawa, K.S. and Shankar, U. (2001). Ecology and economics of domestication of non- timber forest products: An illustration of broomgrass in Darjeeling Himalaya. *J Trop For Sci.* 13:171 – 191.

Sharma, E., Rai,S.C. and Sharma,R. (2001). Soil, water and nutrient conservation in mountain farming systems: Case-study from Sikkim Himalaya. *Journal of Environmental Management* 61: 123-135.

Shukla, R.P. and Ramakrishnan, P.S. (1984). Biomass allocation strategies and productivity of tropical trees related to successional status. *For Ecol Manage.* 9:315 – 324.

Shukla, R.P. and Ramakrishnan, P.S. (1986). Architecture and growth strategies of tropical trees in relation to successional status. *J Ecol.* 74:33 – 46.

Singh, R., Monika, A.and Feroze,S.M. (2013). Minor Forest Product and Marketing: A Case Study of Broom Grass in Meghalaya. *Indian Forester,* 139: 807-810.

Singh,K.A.,Rai,R.N., and Pradhan,I.P.,(1989). Grow amsilo grass in the NEH region *.Indian Farming* 38(10):270-279.

Srijumpa, N. (2002). Use of some grasses as the substrates for Pleurotus sp. cultivation.*Thai Agricultural Research Manual,* 20 (1): 3-8.

Stapleton, C. (1989). Chirang Hill Irrigation Project Damphu: Identification of Bamboos and Potential for Incorporating the Planting of Bamboos into Existing and Possible Activities. Taba: Forestry Research Division.

Sudshishri, S., Dass, A. and Lenka N.K. (2008). Efficacy of vegetative barriers for rehabilitation of degraded hill slopes in eastern India. *Soil and Tillage Research,* 99(1): 98-107.

Thapa, B., Sinclair, F.L., and Walker, D.H. (1995). Incorporation of indigenous knowledge and perspectives in agroforestry development. Part Two: Case-study on the impact of explicit representation of farmers' knowledge. *Agroforestry Systems* 30: 249-261

Thapa, B., Walker, D.H. and Sinclair, F.L. (1997). Indigenous knowledge of the feeding value of tree fodder. *Animal Feed Science and Technology* 67: 97-114

Thorne, P.J., Subba, D.B., Walker, D.H., Thapa, B., Wood, C.D. and Sinclair, F.L. (1999). The basis of indigenous knowledge of tree fodder quality and its implications for improving the use of tree fodder in developing countries. *Animal Feed Science and Technology* 81: 119-131

Tiwari, B.K., Tripathi, R.S. and Barik,S.K. (1995). Broomstick plantation in Meghalaya: A success story. Shillong (India): Regional Centre National Afforestation and Eco-Development Board, North-Eastern Hill University. p. 20.

Tiwari, B.K. (2000). Non-timber forests produce of North East India. *J Hum Ecol.* 11:445 – 455.

Tiwari, B.K. (2001). Domestication of three non-traditional species by shifting cultivators of north-east India. In: International Fund for Agricultural Development, International Development Research Center, Cornell International Institute for Food, Agriculture and Development, International Center for Research in Agroforestry and International Institute of Rural Reconstruction. Shifting cultivation-towards sustainability and resource conservation in Asia. Cavite (Philippines): *IIRR Publisher.* pp. 98–104

Tiwari, B.K. (2014). Broom grass: Its cultivation and production economic in Meghalaya. *Manjari,* 1(1): 7-8.

Tiwari, B.K. and Kumar, C.(2008). Forest products of Meghalaya: Present status and future perspective. Shillong (India): Regional Centre National Afforestation and Eco- Development Board, North-Eastern Hill University.

Tiwari, B.K., Shukla, R.P., Lynser, M.B. and Tynsong, H. (2012). Growth pattern, production, and marketing of *Thysanolaena maxima* (Roxb.) Kuntze: An important non- timber forest product of Meghalaya, India. *Forests, Trees and Livelihoods,* 21 (3): 176–187.

Torrey, J. G., and Clarkson, D. J., (1975).The Development and Function of Roots: Third Cabot Symposium. Academic Press, London, New York, San Francisco.

Walker, D.H., Thorne, P.J., Sinclair, F.L., Thapa, B., Wood, C.D. and Subba, D.B. (1999) A systems approach to comparing indigenous and scientific knowledge: consistency and discriminatory power of indigenous and laboratory assessment of the nutritive value of tree fodder. *Agricultural Systems* 62: 87-103

Yimyong, S., Sangwantanaroj, U. and Punnapayak, H. (2005). Use of weeds for the production of cellulose and ethanol. 1st International Conference on Fermentation Technology for Value Added Agricultural Products. Khon Kaen, Thailand,pp. P-NF21.

Zu,Y.Q.,Li,Y.,Chen,J.J.,Chen,H.Y.,Qin,L.,&Schvartz, C. (2005). Hyperaccumulation of Pb, Zn, and Cd in herbaceous grown on lead-zinc mining area inYunnan, China. Env ironmental Interna tiona l, 31 , 755–762.